THE INVISIBLE MENDER

THE INVISIBLE MENDER

Sarah Maguire

CAPE POETRY

First published 1997

1 3 5 7 9 10 8 6 4 2

© Sarah Maguire 1997

Sarah Maguire has asserted her right
under the Copyright, Designs and Patents Act 1988
to be identified as the author of this work

First published in the United Kingdom in 1997 by Jonathan Cape,
Random House, 20 Vauxhall Bridge Road, London SW1V 2SA

Random House Australia (Pty) Limited
20 Alfred Street, Milsons Point, Sydney,
New South Wales 2061, Australia

Random House New Zealand Limited
18 Poland Road, Glenfield,
Auckland 10, New Zealand

Random House South Africa (Pty) Limited
Box 2263, Rosebank 2121, South Africa

Random House UK Limited Reg. No. 954009

A CIP catalogue record for this book
is available from the British Library

Papers used by Random House UK Limited are natural,
recyclable products made from wood grown in sustainable forests.
The manufacturing processes conform to the environmental
regulations of the country of origin.

ISBN 0 224 04423 0

Typeset by Palimpsest Book Production Limited,
Polmont, Stirlingshire
Printed and bound in Great Britain by
Creative Print and Design (Ebbw Vale) Wales

FOR MY MUM AND DAD

CONTENTS

ACKNOWLEDGEMENTS

Grateful acknowledgement is made to the editors of the *London Review of Books* and *Poetry Review* in which some of these poems were published. 'The Hearing Cure' was written for the fiftieth anniversary of Mind, the mental health charity, and published in *Mind Readings: Writers' Journeys Through Mental States* edited by Sara Dunn, Blake Morrison and Michèle Roberts (London; Minerva, 1996). 'Communion' and 'The Invisible Mender (My First Mother)' were published in *Making for Planet Alice* edited by Maura Dooley (Newcastle Upon Tyne; Bloodaxe Books, 1997). 'Mahbouba Zaidi's Hands' was awarded a small prize in the 1991 National Poetry Competition.

The version of *Wires* by Marina Tsvetaeva printed here was translated from the Russian by Catriona Kelly. I am deeply indebted to Catriona for her patient and attentive scholarly advice, and for her enthusiasm for our collaboration. I would also like to thank Maura Dooley for commissioning me to write a version of part VIII of *Wires*, with Catriona Kelly, for Poetry International in 1992.

I am very grateful for the bursary given to me by the Arts Council of Great Britain which enabled me to complete this book.

I

SWIMMING TO SPINALONGA

through the worst March snowstorm
anyone on this train has ever heard of –
Water Street in Bridgeport, Connecticut
is stopped, a quilt of ice –
only the restless and the homeless
risk the streets tonight.

This train, like any train
I've ever taken anywhere,
moves from metropolis to detritus,
its trajectory –
from dressed-stone, steel-clad, po-mo vaults,
heated, peopled, electronic,

to those laid-off warehouses,
their tall machines eviscerated,
left to breed a skin of verdigris
against the open, negligent air –
is voodoo economics stripped:
the counting-houses, gilts and deals

are come to this,
a rusting chain-link fence
around an empty lot,
two huge cogs lying out of gear,
fabulously swollen with the snow.
The stilled train

creaks a little to itself, then leaves
New Haven, all but two carriages
plunged into darkness
(there now are nine of us),
the steady veil of snow
covering our tracks, clinging to

the gargoyle icicles that rope-
off the carriages, glaze the metal stairway
with a skid of glass.
I don't know where I am.
I can only match the cold-occluded signposts
with the Amtrack schedule in my lap,

to plot this journey to new weather.
Two hours ago we left Penn Station,
tunnelling through Manhattan,
then emerged – where? –
was that the Bronx below me?
the rigid grid of houses

grilled into the distance
by a futuristic blueprint years ago.
Nothing balks this weather:
the heedless, desperate cars
abandoned, slewed across
the streets at random,

their gases and their deadly engines
made benign by sheaves of whiteness.
This is not a pastoral.
The snug, urbane, well-heated
Amtrack train I'm travelling in
mechanically performs its engineering feats:

balancing these thousand tons of metal,
plastic, humans, glass
across a cantilevered iron bridge
forged a century ago,
behind which fumes a power station
sixty metres high, one huge wall a window

4

golden, molten, transfigured by its power.
Electricity. Its nineteenth–century
narrative of hope for some
is giving out.
How many of the houses
that I pass above are dark from choice?

On the local news they showed
a welfare family disconnected,
in the dark, abjured, their tv screen
just slackened glass
but for reflections of their hollowed faces
that the lighting cameraman

threw onto the dead machine.
The cold comes down.
The journey from James Watts' boiled kettle
to this insulated Amtrack train
seems evolutionary, tracked and planned.
I read the signs but don't know where I am.

Outside there is a bonfire in a parking lot,
a group of cold men pressed together
round its light.

THE MARYLAND STATE PENITENTIARY

For three nights I have slept in a room
with a view of the Maryland State Penitentiary.

That huge cathedral of punishment
holds its bulk against the winter storm,

its thickened walls immune to snow, to cold,
the falling snow small flurries

in the steady yellow floodlights,
their untroubled gaze

fixing on the big walls and the bars,
one gothic window tall enough for prayer.

My window also has its bars –
wrought-iron, sculpted, almost elegant –

to keep the outside out.
The frozen metal burns my palms.

*

A year ago I worked Inside.
The night I left,

I stood in the abandoned Education Block
and breathed in that sour, cooped-up air.

I memorised the worn-down walls,
the braggadocio and the insults carved on desks,

before I locked those dank and straitened rooms.
In the narrow corridor

I pressed my face against the filthy, meshed-in windows
to stare at a view that would not change:

the half-demolished prisoner-of-war-camp buildings
jutting concrete, wires, mesh and rusted bars

out into the weather.
Then I wandered through the deserted, darkened prison,

unlocked, then locked, the heavy gates six times,
handed in my keys, and left.

*

Tonight in Baltimore
I slip the latch and let the cold come in

to see if I can see a window that a prisoner could see through –
to watch the storm come down

or, if gazing at the city spread beneath him,
could glimpse this small and distant building

these red-brick walls, my tiny square of light,
almost hidden

by the endless, falling, freezing flakes of snow.

COMMUNION

I

We both might wonder what you're doing here
till you take refuge from your hunger in my fridge
and then come out with something

that we share the name for: *choriço picante*.
I watch you pierce
the raw meat with a fork

and hold it in the naked ring of gas
until the skin is charred and blistered black
until the stove enamel's measled red.

Slit it down the side
and open out its bleeding heart –
ruddy, vivid, rough.

II

We cannot speak each other's tongue
and so you open up your shirt
to give me signs, to show your wounds.

I know this much:
that, as a child, you fled to Lisbon from Luanda
with a bayonet wound a foot long

(never sutured)
that now grows on your arm
as though a snake's embossed there;

that your skin was punched with shot
which, ten years later, form the dark stigmata
branded on your legs and arms.

III

Take this pungent flesh into your mouth
and staunch your hunger.
Eat.

slip into mine. She leans me against
a smooth, cool pillar
and takes my waist in her arm.

Her hair is in my eyes. Her dry brow against
my lips. We have walked at midnight
along slim paths of plaited stone,

leaving the streetlights for darkness.
The other tourists are asleep. The Sicilians are dreaming.
My palm traces the muscles of walls

softened by a millennium of palms and shoulders.
Her hip presses into my hip. Her spine is under
my fingers. She leads me through Érice

to the Castello de Vénere. I want to tell her
that Daedalus came here, bringing a honeycomb
of gold for Aphrodite, honouring her shrine,

but there is nothing between us save broken
Italian, schoolgirl French. I understand
how she will come here at dusk

and lean out into the still, aromatic air, searching
for Africa, for a glimpse of the rim of her home:
a dim, glaucous haze sixty miles distant,

a continent away. Tonight there is nothing but blackness
and stars. Later she will lead me to the hotel
and slip in through the back. *Rosa*

the owner calls out, asking where she has been.
They have changed her name. *Hush*, she whispers,
It's far too complex.

SWIMMING TO SPINALONGA

for Crispin

At dusk I watched you swim to Spinalonga.
Sitting in the bar at Plaka

I felt the glass of ouzo
cool against my palms;

the hard ice loosened,
bled the liquor white,

until its clarity had turned opaque,
until I held a glass of milky quartz.

I looked up and you were yards out,
your sleek head

a needle
suturing the navy waters.

Along the shore
big granite pebbles

exhaled the whole day's heat
like fresh loaves just tipped from the tin.

The tamarisk tree kept its own counsel,
its dense laced fronds

harbouring a coolness
all day long. For half an hour I lose you.

The sickle moon's no use,
her paltry beam

illuminating nothing but her bony self,
and Spinalonga island is a distant darkness.

Forty years ago I would have looked upon
an awkward constellation of small lights,

pinpointing deportation,
the bright stigmata

of the colony of lepers
banished there,

these calming waters
a no-man's-land they died to cross.

The place has been cleaned out now:
the disinfectant room,

the cisterns and the laundry
no longer function.

Three days ago
I took refuge from the fevered sun

inside the old taverna,
its walls undone,

the plaster flayed right back
to rotted slats,

the roof defeated.
But away from glare and weather

was a frieze of cobalt blue,
the intricate flowers and fruits

were steadfast
where the stones had met and held together.

I took the rusted window clasp and pushed
the shutters back: in the courtyard

a cuckoo Yucca
bulked against the garden walls.

I found you at the graveyard,
the tombstones shattered

exposing whitened skulls,
the longbones

of four hundred lepers
whose journey ended here.

The night comes on:
small stars of jasmine

let go their piercing scent.
I watch the dark sea gather

and relax,
then find its rhythm is you swimming back to me.

Climbing from the water to dry land,
you paint the grey stones inky

shaking off your skinful
of the salty sea.

THE MUSLIM QUARTER

for Izzat Ghazzawi

The Old City unspools behind me
    as I slip down the Suq Khan ez-Zeit
        close as a shadow to a hand.

Sallow lamps pool on the ceiling
    threading me down
        to the bottom of light.

The markets have been closed for the night;
    the stalls' rusted doors
        belted and padlocked,

the cabinets of objects concertina'd
    and concealed.
        Cheek by jowl

sleep dustpans and dresses
    and dolls that blink,
        crockery, suitcases,

razorblades and prayer mats,
    oil, olive oil, and olive-oil soap.
        Tucked up, packed up,

mouths stitched shut.
    The vaulted roof gives way
        to a canopy of milky glass,

fine wrought iron finishing the panes.
    Through a crack the stars fall in,
        the heedless stars

dazzling in their freezing orbits.
I feel my way
down a corridor of silence

trying to imagine these are buildings
ordinary, useful and at rest
as eighteen soldiers

watch me cross the Via Dolorosa.
The Day of Atonement is finished.
Even as I turn

and walk back to the East
the Tunnel is dug out
under my feet.

Jerusalem, 23rd September 1996 (Yom Kippur)

II

WIRES

by Marina Tsvetaeva

The waves of the heart would not foam up so beautifully,
they would turn straight to spirits, if the old dumb cliff of
Fate did not stand in their way.

Hölderlin, Empedokles

This hot-line sings along the pylons fixing up the skies:
across the highest fiery heights of heaven
I'm wiring you my burnt-out tithe of ash and dust.

From street to street – down tracks of sighs
the signal's coupled from pole to pole –
–I–lo–ve–you . . .

I'm begging you (enough dead letters –
I'm too wired-up for writing lines).

This grid of pylons rigs the static sky
that Atlas heaved upon his back – and
the sports-track where Atalanta out-ran every man . . .
The signal comes from pole to pole: Goo–ood–bye . . .

Listen to the last cracked static
from my gutted throat: For–gi–ive–me . . .

These pylons rig the fields and seas
sing the pacific Atlantic trade lines –
they're flying higher, higher –
but I've crossed lines with Ariadne – Come back!

Turn back – Don't leave me banged-up
in this hell-on-earth with no parole!
The line is going dead
with all the keening of lost souls.

For–pi–ty's–sa–ake! These steel wires
steal me, seal me off –
Can you hear me call you
through this seething, shrieking swarm?

through the cut-dead howl
of Eurydice's searing passion?
Her last call gargling through
thick ducts of mud: A–la–as . . .

17. iii. 1923

II

How can I break through to you? My hot veins boil
against this chain of poesy, these throttling rhymes.
I'm telling you all poetry, all tragedy –
Racine or Shakespeare – 's far too dainty for my anguish.

They weep. They bleed. The sweet rose hides a snake.
But Phaedra ranted for a boy (her son-in-law at that!)
and Ariadne went insane for faithless Theseus.
I suffer more. I lack a tragic ending.

This inferno has no rim, no name, no signposts – no degree.
I've lost count of simple numbers. Losing you I lose
the possible, the probable – all the things that never happened
slide down into unbeing. Null. Minus. Dead.

How can I live if each breath I take's inspired by you?
If each particle and molecule of air is made of you?
Break my bones, you'll find the sands of Naxos Ariadne wept
    upon.
Cut my veins, and through them flows the black infernal Styx.

This miasmic vanity is bottomless, I know, but nothing's real –
(though sometimes I do know that I'm not Ariadne).
I close my eyes and see hallucinations, open them and I'm
    deluded.
Look – even the date on this calendar's a fabrication –

like you are – aren't you? (Am I really cracking up?)
Oh, name me the oceans, show me the cities where I can
search for you (the sightless seeking the invisible).
Now listen to the sound waves wiring you my last farewell.

Washed up against this lonely post, heartbroken, I break down
and weep . . .

18. iii. 1923

III

Everything's upside down – I've turned out the lot
(you're way out of sight, so semaphore's hopeless) –
I'm calling on caterwauling (a whole chorus) to help me:

so listen to my break – my shameless solo,
my flying colours, my fireworks – I'm getting high –
can you hear my torch song singeing all the wires?

Sad telegraph poles – these wires they carry never touch –
but while the cold stars shine above them
they're wiring you my soul so palpable you'll taste my broken
    lips.

As long as this scorched earth beneath our feet is soil
as long as wild nights ebb to dawn
I shall chain you, fix you, wire you – heart to heart.

I'm wiring you through cataclysms, revolutions, acts of God,
through all the rigged, fixed, trumped-up lies –
my smothered cries, my wild – my savage passion.

Those mortal wires strung out against the sky may rust and twist
but mine is fixed – and I'll break through to you
till sound waves turn to water, till light years fade away.

19. iii. 1923

way off the beat   we've gone beyond the pale
the ghetto's all wired up

I'm burned up   turned on   flying so high
my guts are strung out   pluck me and I'll cry out
my heart's so beat up   it's sprung the rhythm
I've stunned the metre out of time

you know I'm too off-beat for common time
so swing it all you want   but you can't beat Time
that dead beat is dead meat
just give up whistling in the dark

Sss! I've got you wired!
soon it's going to strike you like a smack in the face
I'm going haywire   forgive these hard lines
I want to give it to you straight

like a nightingale in no-man's-land
my song wastes into the wilderness
I'm beaten by the fine-strung lyre of your fingers
by the full wet fruit of your lips   open like a girl's

20. iii. 1923

V

I'm not a witch – and this isn't black magic!

I've picked up every trick that exists
in those white books – to get you
At the bitter ends of the earth – I shall reach you
My anguish – my passion – my siren song – summons you

From my eyrie watchtower – the world's at my feet
Ships cast anchor – unfurl their sails in the blood-red sunset
I'll disembowel all the bottomless oceans to find you
From the vaults of the earth I shall raise you on high

No Passion exceeds mine – no martyrdom's sweeter
Heartbroken – in pieces – I'm everywhere –
in sun rise and gold mines – in wheat fields and weeping
I am alpha and omega – I am and I will be –
and I will claim your lips – as God claims a soul

Mouth to mouth – you inspire me
I'll fight through the eye of the finest needle
I'll gatecrash purgatory – endure inquisition
my penitent lips ripped open by thorns
At the very last gasp – I'll grab you from the grave

Give up – this isn't a song
Give up – you're shot down in flames
Give up – lay down your arms
From these open arms there is no escape

Mouth to mouth I inspire you (My breasts harden
my eye-lids are sealed – my lips turn to stone)
Like the Witch of Endor – I'll summons the dead
I'll blackmail the living – till all hell's broken loose

Don't think I don't know you've another beside you
But on Judgement Day the fight isn't fixed – Now watch me
   get high!
I am and I will be and I will claim your soul
Pax! – *this* kiss of peace chains lips to lips

25. iii. 1923

VI

And now: the gods are on high
as gifts mount up from hand to hand.

And now: I'm descending the mountain
as insight begins to dawn on the mountain.

And now: the cards are all blank
as good intentions mount in a circle.

And now: my eyes can't see my hands
as sight begins to dawn in the soul.

25. iii. 1923

VII

And when my beloved brother
walked past the last elm tree
(their branches like arms – waving and waving)
there were more tears than there were eyes

And when my beloved friend
turned the last corner
(a wall made of cries – calling and calling)
there were more waves than there were hands

As though hands fled from their arms just to follow you
as though lips – casting spells – fled in your wake
Speech leaves me – dumb
Bones leave me – handless

And when my beloved – (dear God! don't forsake me!)
there were more tears than there were eyes
more eyes than there were stars
fixed over the cold Atlantic

26. iii. 1923

VIII

as patiently as tarmac is worn down to bedrock
as patiently as a consumptive wastes into death
as patiently as rumours are pieced into news
as patiently as the wronged savour their vengeance:

that's how I'll wait for you (my hands laced into stillness –
just like a kept boy waits on his mistress)
as patiently as a poet listens for a rhyme
as patiently as nails are bitten right down to the quick:

that's how I'll wait for you (my eyes cast on the dirt,
my lips sealed, and my teeth wired together)
as patiently as indolence slides into voluptuousness
as patiently as beads are strung into place –

– a car door slams – my heart slams back –
a letter shoots through the door, boiling up a storm –
like a news flash that warns me:
'The junta has fallen. We must take to the streets'

I'm out of here

27. iii. 1923

IX

Spring makes us sleepy: let's doze
All distances are dissolved by: sleep
All separations are sutured by: sleep
All day I dream that I'll dream you all night

God knows who lies with whom
God knows who lies to whom
God knows who'll share in my sorrow
God knows who'll take on this torment

My grief is the grief of a soul lost in eternity
My grief is the grief of a motherless child
My grief is the grief of a prisoner in solitary

Memory slips through the fingers
like sand through glass
All the seats have been taken
All the hearts rented out

My life now means 'life'
A sentence without love
I'm condemned without love to the archive of love
to turn all the dry pages from dawn until dusk

Our love is as dumb as grass threading the soil
as ore veining the far caves of a mountain
as dumb as the plot of a natural disaster
our love is as dumb as: water

Listen to the sound of them stitching our shroud:
slavery   slavery   slavery

5. iv. 1923

X

Day after day, as you quicken inside her
I shall be with you

The world is full of me
My doubles possess you

Remember me as a rope made of sand
Remember me as a heart cast in stone

Remember me in the keening of the wind
Hear my voice when a stranger cries out in her sleep

Find me under the city
where the homeless throng –

recognise that shawl
tightened against the cold?

– recognise that shroud
burned-up in hell?

Come closer!
under those skirts beats

– the miracle of life:
I bring you a child!

More awesome than a first-born
more fearsome than Rachel

My song is immortal!
All flesh is: dust

11. iv. 1923

III

NURSERY PRACTICES

MY GRAFTING KNIFE

A whole week's wages
balanced on my palm

The cherrywood clasp
burnished and finished with brass

Lockjaw
I unjoint the heart

and the steel heart
arcs

from silver to blue
hurting the air

The fine blade cleaves
to the whetstone

first a dry rasp grates
the granular carborundum

then the whispered finesse
of the oilstone filmed with oil

Six strops on the leather strap
I could carve

scarves of gossamer tissue
One poised gesture

and the ichor oozes
The knife stop – my right thumb

crisscrossed with hair-scars
tarnished with sap

NO. 3 GREENHOUSE, 7.30 a.m.

Genuflect
crossing the threshold

The unopened air
heady with the odours
of cloves and roses

The carnations are speechless
Candles
ascending the nave

(So easy to befuddle –
remember ink in the jamjar
the pinked frills taking blue)

They must lose their heads
before they turn spray

I stub out the buds
A twist and they're single

Auxins surge from the one heady flower
the bouquet's darling

Cloistered in glass
I am taken by ritual
postulant to the blooms

THE GROWING ROOM

Lux eterna
the Dutch lamps
beam all night

Walls of loam
shelved in green trays

Dicotyledons
breaking the surface

dense as a rain-forest
glimpsed from a plane

Begonia seeds
are costlier than gold

I tweezer open
the cellophane envelope

unhouse the blond dust
inhale

then waft
the precious cirrus

softly
down to earth

THE MIST BENCH

Even at night, at random
a click
– and mist fumes

from the watchtowers
clouding the cuttings
with fog

Bare leaves are downy
turn blurred
and glaucous

as the fine fur plumps
and sleeves itself
with water

Ten beats and it's
finished
The electric leaf

buried in the leaves
is parched
and replenished

all night

YEAR-ROUND CHRYSANTHEMUMS

In mid-July
they think it is winter

All it takes
is an hour's incandescence

at midnight
and their day

germinates: twenty-four hours
makes two

Year-round chrysanthemums
the long nights

make you rich
and fecund

Your bunched, curled faces
magenta and saffron

phototropic with desire
inexorably riding the light

WATERSHED

Overnight, *Bellis perennis*
would heave its fist of leaves
up into the light
rupturing the bowling green.

In the flat heat of the afternoon
I knelt in my small shadow
puncturing the hard earth
with a dinner fork,

attempting to unseat
the urchin daisy from its home,
its nude roots woven in the soil,
the pink-flushed blooms

slim embryos, packed within
the tight-whorled leaves;
then I tucked the new seeds in
to mend the wounded soil.

This was the summer
when you could fill your palm
with grass seeds
and I'd know their names:

Festuca rubra commutata
(Chewing's fescue)
Festuca rubra rubra
(strong creeping red)

and *Agrostis tenuis*,
its gentle growth as fine
as baby's hair.
It never rained.

The longest drought since
records began. All July
the tight sky banged above us
all day long.

My reddened shoulders
turned to skin; detached;
a loose, translucent parchment
that streamed off,

frayed, and blossomed
in my twisted sheets
as dust. At work
I learned to use

the Ransome's Auto-Certes;
each week my boss would tinker
with it upside down,
tickling the carburettor,

feeding slips of cartridge paper
into the hive of sharpened blades
until it sliced them
into perfect squares.

Three times
he let me carve the lawn
into its warp and weft,
the shaven grass striped green,

then lighter green,
then green again.
No girl has ever done that,
he told me, when I stopped for tea.

Some of the Bowling Club
are blaming you for this –
he gestured at the sickening lawn.
My sex could blight

their turf. Turn milk
foetid in an hour.
It never rained. By August
we were mowing down the soil.

We gave up watering after eight:
the moisture either dropped
straight through the ground,
or simply turned to steam;

so I rose at four,
watched Venus slip
behind a block of flats,
and left for work.

The dawn released the fragrance
of the lime-flower trees
which cloaked the long,
cool avenue I walked along;

the half-light lifted,
the distant trees, the lawns,
first grey, then glaucous;
the bowling green,

the porter's lodge now
breaking into form.
It never rained. I learned
the fungal sicknesses

of turf by heart:
Fairy Rings, Fusarium patch
(its pink mycelia
like cotton wool)

and red thread
(corticum disease);
in the half-light
of the musty shed

gleamed poisonous tins
of malachite green
to wipe them out.
The *Salix tortuosa*

lost its leaves and died;
its twisted branches
made an absent *haiku*
against the naked wall.

Only the Giant Hogweed
thrived, spawning
by the putrid riverbank,
its bloated umbels

carried twelve-foot high
by hollow stems,
hairy and maculate,
harbouring a vicious juice,

cousin to the Hemlock
and to Cowbane, to the deadly
Hemlock Water Dropwort.
It never rained.

Each night at home
I found the small rooms
stiff with heat,
the hard air

tight against the glass.
I was nineteen. Waiting
for the sky to open.
I washed my shirt

and watched it dry
from navy into sapphire
in an afternoon.
Across the estate

two dogs were fighting.
I heard the ice-cream van,
the children I no longer
recognised clamouring

outside the flats.
No one called all weekend.
I slept through Sunday.
That night I climbed

the ten flights to the roof
and out onto the flat
expanse of asphalt.
It warmed my back.

I had never seen
so many stars,
so old, so far away,
shining down

their messages of light
from centuries ago.
I didn't know
the constellations,

I lacked the skill
to make the stars reveal
their names and myths –
until one

slid then hurtled
down the sky. Next day
the floods came down.

IV

THE INVISIBLE MENDER

TIDEMARKS

The seaside out of season: it's pissing down.
At equinoctial low spring tide the beach is nude,
the rocks stripped back,
barnacles left sucking at the air.

These ordinary limestone extrusions
are salt-dark from their dealings with the tides,
are rimed with spiralwrack and thongweed,
pitted into rockpools;

and, the one I'm mirrored in's
a small home
to a solitary sea anemone
shrugging its undulant, rose-hued fronds for food.

Rounding the headland twenty years late
nothing has changed,
only the cedar of Lebanon has stretched to shield
the red-brick crenellated miners' rest home

from the restless waves.
The posh hotel has held its corner;
next, the stolid row of big
bay-fronted bed-and-breakfasts

curves down to the front.
Months ago, the heath was burnt;
and now the tarmacadamed path
bisects the heather, gorse and broom

the startled undershrubs caught petrified,
their gestured arms in flight,
wrought and blackened by the heat.
Further on fresh shoots break through,

the yellow lips of gorse blooms
easing through the burl of spines,
the fine pelt coated with the salty rain.
The scorched earth smells of artichoke.

At seventeen I hadn't seen an artichoke.
Nowadays I've learnt the ritual
of stripping back the tight-packed petalled head
to unsleeve the longed-for heart,

and to abjure the feathered needles of the choke,
its iris tempting and implacable.
At seventeen I wondered why
the sand below me

slipped beyond the small vocabulary
I tried to dress it in
of platinum and mushroom, oyster, eau-de-Nil –
till dusk fell and the tide drew in

to wash the shades away.
In the cupboard on the stairs at home
a Huntley and Palmers biscuit tin
is labelled 'minerals' in my cursive, adolescent hand.

I opened it last week
and found I knew each rock,
its journey and geography, each given name –
feldspar, jasper, tourmaline or quartz –

carefully printed
then stuck down with strips of yellowed sellotape
the decades have transformed
into another mineral –

mica, isinglass,
the lifted texture of an insect's wing.
And now I trace myself across the sands
away from crowds and relatives

searching for the certainties of crystallography.
I find the place I prised a vein
of milky quartz
out from its bed of carboniferous limestone,

its cold hexagonals
opalescent, almost perfect,
each crystal spawned from an ideal form,
its flawed, unkiltered rhomboids

made opaque by slip and circumstance,
so knowable and mineral and hard
against my palm.
In books of crystallography I found

its history, its structure and its family
reduced to letters, numbers, symbols
that evaded me.
I dreamt of schist and basalt,

malachite, obsidian and marble, jet;
undressed each landscape to its geomorphic curves,
saw glaciers and slow moraines
ease the valleys opened, fertile, wet,

drumlins scattering in their wake.
I knew the sucking clay of London
dropped beneath my feet.
One day I would be mineral,

my cold bones leached of flesh and hair
crumbling into soil.
I came here out of season once before,
my Irish grandpa with one green eye and one blue

was dead, and I sat out the funeral on this bench
seeking comfort in these cliffs and headlands,
the loved, familiar bay,
the flux of its geology

incremental, fixed, beyond my mortal eyes –
not knowing I'd return two decades on,
sit down here and take in this landscape,
collect myself, then walk on in the rain.

HEAVENLY BODY

I could stake out the summer at my kitchen window:
    scanning the street,

searching for the scarlet flare of your Mercedes at my kerb.
    Since St Swithin's Day

it's pelted down. On August 12th the world's astronomers
    observed the Perseids,

expectant that Swift-Tuttle's comet dust would storm
    to starlight.

But in Notting Hill the clouds occlude the heavens;
    the passing cars

in darkness turn anaemic, their lights a sallow blur
    along the seething road.

PROOF

Your abandoned bottle of Russkaya vodka lies in my icebox,
cold as a gun; it will chill but not freeze,
the slow distillation latent beneath the iced glass.

PSORIASIS

After all this time on my knees
I am starting to bleed –

the cushion, the dark sheets
are foxed with my dead skin

worn from love
from the way you move me,

the cream dust like meal,
spoor in the tracks.

Again you kneel back
to look at me like this

opened before you, patient
your hand encircling my ankle.

It has rained all afternoon,
the light fretting of water on glass

seeps into my breathing,
your musk on my lips.

I lay my cheek on the pillow
to take you in

I could be a child again
suckling my own thumb.

DUST

I hold the condom to the light
the still-warm cells seething and dividing

There's a bleached aroma with a rim of zinc
– like a sixpence hidden in your mouth

In ten days time
the thickened lining of my womb

will loosen, turn to blood
between my legs

A decade more of this
and then I'm finished

Cells are leaving my body
the fine dust in the sheets

the grey dust on the high shelves
the lampshade

the mauve dust ravelling into nests
under the stairs, by my old winter shoes

pollen on the windowpane
as the maculate sky gives in to dusk

THE INVISIBLE MENDER (MY FIRST MOTHER)

I'm sewing on new buttons
to this washed silk shirt.
Mother-of-pearl,
I chose them carefully.
In the haberdashers on Chepstow Place
I turned a boxful over
one by one,
searching for the backs with flaws:
those blemished green or pink or aubergine,
small birthmarks on the creamy shell.

These afternoons are short,
the sunlight buried after three or four,
sap in the cold earth.
The trees are bare.
I'm six days late.
My right breast aches so
when I bend to catch a fallen button
that strays across the floor.
Either way,
there'll be blood on my hands.

Thirty-seven years ago you sat in poor light
and sewed your time away,
then left.
But I'm no good at this:
a peony of blood gathers on my thumb, falls
then widens on the shirt like a tiny, opening mouth.

I think of you like this –
as darkness comes,
as the window that I can't see through

is veiled with mist
which turns to condensation
slipping down tall panes of glass,
a mirror to the rain outside –
and I know that I'll not know
if you still are mending in the failing light,
or if your hands (as small as mine)
lie still now, clasped together, underground.

THE HEARING CURE

I dunk my head
    under water
and come up
    deaf. My left ear

solid, as though
    half the world
is moored in perspex.
    My life

bifurcates. I turn
    around
and a jellied stillness
    drags behind me,

an abeyance of rustling,
    mortality hushed.
The rope of blood
    twists

in my ear, plaiting
    and unplaiting,
the world gone
    bone.

Each night
    the slow wax silts
into place
    coagulating sibilance,

muffling sussuration,
    the soft moraine
lagging the tympanum,
    secluding

stirrup, hammer, anvil
in a distant room.
The plug is full.
When I was three

sound turned to stone,
then festered;
my skull became
a labyrinth of pain,

my taut throat
stuffed
with liquid needles.
That winter afternoon

you pushed my cot
into the warm front room
and soothed me on your lap.
There was the red wool

of your jumper
unravelling
at one wrist,
your kind heart

marking time. By tea
it was dark outside;
the football results
came on the radio;

Scottish League Division Two –
Stirling Albion,
Cowdenbeath,
Montrose, Arbroath,

Dunfermline,
       Heart of Midlothian,
Queen of the South —
       a litany

that lulled me
       into sleep.
I left you
       twenty years ago.

Since then
       we've hardly talked —
until I found you
       shrunken, frightened,

speechless
       on a geriatric ward,
your legs gone dead
       from grief.

You couldn't stand it
       when your brother died.
And now you cling to me
       for dear life,

your wasted,
       beautiful hands
slim messengers of fear.
       Weeks on,

you start to tell me things
       I've never heard before,
all that silence
       frozen in your limbs.

61

But when we got you home
        we found
they hadn't bathed you
        for a month

because you'd not complain,
        not ask, not bother anyone.
It made me sick.
        And now I'm ill, bewildered,

lonely – and I know
        you'll never make me better
any more. I feed
        the warmed sweet almond oil

with a dropper
        into my dead ear
and feel the good oil
        opening the wax.

In four days time
        I'll hold
the white enamel kidney bowl
        against my neck

while the huge syringe
        shoots water
down the auditory canal.
        At first it thrums

like a far-off city
        and then the whole live ocean
rushes in.
        Afterwards,

in the warm November dusk,
     I sat in the park
and watched two bats
     suturing

the darkening air,
     their zigzag flight
latticing the stark
     and emptying trees

with a fragile network,
     an impossible filigree
that fails
     as it describes

their hunger close to night.
     Their sight is sound –
those high-pitched cries
     light up the chestnut trees

with call and echo,
     making feeling
from reflection.
     And I can hear them!

There, right at the edge
     of sound,
like a quill on glass,
     an exquisite engraving

that I thought
     I'd lost forever.
I raise my fingers
     and I rub them

near my mended ear
    to hear that precious music,
the pitch of flesh
    on flesh.

THE INSTRUMENT REPAIRER

Your sax in hock for six weeks
now lies in pieces on the floor,
mouthpiece, crook, body and bell.

This is the exploded view.
The tubing, the unsheathed rods
spilled onto the carpet
in a Chinese augury,

the homeless keys,
pieces of eight
patient for discovery,

all strewn around the empty body,
its tone holes speechless
next their crown of thorns –

the shock of the key-springs
bristling from each post –
long thorns on a thorn bush
out of bloom.

Even the skin is wounded,
the tarnished brass
fuscous and bronzed,

foxed with verdigris
by the seeping acids
of spit and sweat.

And these are your tools –
a surgeon's palette
arrayed at your side –

mandrils, swaging tools,
reevers and burnishers,
planishing hammers smaller
than a tool in a doll's house.

For two days
rain stipples the window
as you balance and hone,

recorking the neck pipe,
tapping the dents smooth,
then seating each pad

with shellac and a flame
till the fluorescent leak-light
shows no leak.

Your shaved reed dilates
in a tooth-glass,
swelling with moisture

as, piece by piece,
with key guards and touch felts
you remember the body,
till your Selmer VI is whole.

NOTES

Wires is a free adaptation (or Lowellian 'imitation') of Marina Tsvetaeva's lyric cycle of ten poems, *Provoda*, which was written in 1923 and first published in its complete form in *After Russia (Posle Rossii)* in Paris in 1928.

The sequence was inspired by Tsvetaeva's passionate epistolary relationship with Boris Pasternak which began in June, 1922. 'Tsvetaeva felt she had found in Pasternak,' writes Lily Feiler, 'not only a man she could love and a poet she could admire but a man who could respond to her as a poet and a woman – exactly the kind of illusion that could be kept alive in letters.' Pasternak was, 'Tsvetaeva's image of her poet-twin . . . he was her "brother in the fifth season and the fourth dimension".'

Wires was begun on the day of Pasternak's departure from Berlin for Moscow; although Tsvetaeva was then living in Prague, she experienced Pasternak's return to Russia as an anguishing abandonment of their shared exile. In the cycle, 'Tsvetaeva expressed the pain of their separation. She invoked the passion of Eurydice and Orpheus; she used Ariadne's pain for the absent Theseus to convey her own passion, her own pain.' [Lily Feiler, *Marina Tsvetaeva: The Double Beat of Heaven and Hell* (Durham and London; Duke University Press, 1994; pp. 140–41.)]

Wires depends on a paradox: that of applying the imagery of erotic love to a relationship that was never consummated, as Tsvetaeva and Pasternak did not have an affair. And, as with a great deal of Tsvetaeva's work, the cycle also depends on puns. In *Wires*, most crucially, Tsvetaeva repeatedly makes a connection between the Russian *provoda* ('telegraph wires') and *provody* ('send-off', specifically a farewell party for someone departing on a long journey, going off to war, or being conscripted into the army – or in the sense of 'sending-off' a corpse at a funeral).

My version of *Wires* began as a line-by-line, annotated translation from the Russian by Catriona Kelly – from which I have departed in various ways, attempting to reflect the spirit if not the letter of

Tsvetaeva's original text. In some instances I've replaced references to Russian folklore with material more resonant to contemporary English-speaking readers; and I've also tried to convey both the emotional and linguistic intensity of Tsvetaeva's original through punning on the many meanings of 'wires' and 'wired' in English.

Needless to say, none of this would have been possible without Catriona's help.